Raccoon Cubs

by Ruth Owen

Consultants:
Suzy Gazlay, M.A.
Recipient, Presidential Award
for Excellence in Science Teaching

Leah Birmingham, RVT
Assistant Director
Sandy Pines Wildlife Centre
Napanee, Ontario, Canada

BEARPORT
PUBLISHING

New York, New York

Credits

Cover, © John Blackburn/Shutterstock; 4–5, © age fotostock/Superstock; 6–7, © H. Reinhard/Arco Images/Alamy; 9T, © C.C. Lockwood/Animals Animals; 9B, © Shutterstock; 10, © Carsten Volkwein/Wikipedia (public domain); 11, © Radius/Superstock; 12, © C.C. Lockwood/Bruce Coleman Photography; 13, © Fotosearch/Superstock; 14, © Jurgen & Christine Sohns/FLPA; 15, © Tim Fitzharris/Minden Pictures/FLPA; 16, © Becky Sheridan/Shutterstock; 17, © Danita Delimont/Getty Images; 18–19, © S & D & K Maslowski/FLPA; 20, © Becky Sheridan/Shutterstock; 21, © Scenic Shutterbug/Shutterstock; 22T, © Becky Sheridan/Shutterstock; 22C, © Scenic Shutterbug/Shutterstock; 22B, © Fred Leonero/Shutterstock; 23T, © Shutterstock; 23C, © Shutterstock; 23B, © Shutterstock.

Publisher: Kenn Goin
Editorial Director: Adam Siegel
Creative Director: Spencer Brinker
Design: Alix Wood
Photo Researcher: Ruby Tuesday Books Ltd

Library of Congress Cataloging-in-Publication Data

Owen, Ruth, 1967–
    Raccoon cubs / by Ruth Owen.
        p. cm. — (Wild baby animals)
    Includes bibliographical references and index.
    ISBN-13: 978-1-61772-154-0 (library binding)
    ISBN-10: 1-61772-154-9 (library binding)
    1. Raccoon—Infancy—Juvenile literature. I. Title.
    QL737.C26O94 2011
    599.76'32139—dc22
                                    2010041249

For more information, write to Bearport Publishing Company, Inc., 101 Fifth Avenue, Suite 6R, New York, New York 10003. Printed in the United States of America in North Mankato, Minnesota.

122010
10810CGE

10 9 8 7 6 5 4 3 2 1

Contents

Meet some raccoon cubs

Three baby raccoons are playing in a tree.

The babies are called **cubs**.

Sometimes people call them **kits**.

They live in the tree with their mother.

4

Raccoon cub

What is a raccoon?

A raccoon is an animal about the size of a small dog.

have

The fur around a raccoon's eyes is black.

It looks like a mask.

Thick fur

Mask

North American raccoon

Where do raccoons live?

Many raccoons live in **forests**.

Others live on **farmland**.

Some raccoons live in towns and cities.

The yellow part of this map shows where North American raccoons live.

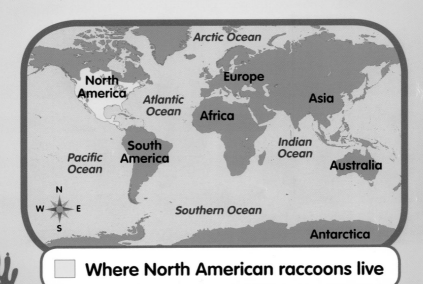

Arctic Ocean

North America

Europe

Asia

Atlantic Ocean

Africa

Pacific Ocean

South America

Indian Ocean

Australia

Southern Ocean

Antarctica

Where North American raccoons live

Raccoon on
a city rooftop

Raccoon homes

Raccoons live in homes called **dens**.

They make dens in holes in trees.

Some raccoons in towns and cities make dens in garages and in the roofs of houses.

Den

Raccoon cubs

A mother raccoon gives birth to her cubs in a den.

She feeds her cubs milk from her body.

Cubs feeding

The cubs cannot see because their eyes are closed.

14-day-old cubs

Time to go outside

After three weeks, the cubs' eyes open.

Now they can see.

When they are about eight weeks old, the cubs go outside.

They play and practice climbing trees.

Finding food

A mother raccoon leaves her den to look for food.

Her cubs go, too.

They must learn how to find food.

Raccoons eat foods such as plants, fruit, eggs, and insects.

They catch fish with their **paws**.

Fish

Paw

Look out for raccoons!

Raccoons look for food around people's homes.

There is usually plenty to eat!

Raccoons tip over trash cans to find food.

Sometimes they steal the nuts that people feed to birds.

Growing up

Cubs leave their mother when they are between six and nine months old.

They know how to make dens.

They know where to look for food.

The cubs are ready to begin their grown-up lives!

Glossary

cubs (KUHBZ) the babies of some animals, such as raccoons, bears, and tigers

dens (DENZ) homes where wild animals can rest, be safe, and have babies

farmland (FARM-land) places where farmers keep animals and grow vegetables and other foods

forests (FOR-ists) places where lots of trees grow

kits (KITS) another name for raccoon cubs

paws (PAWZ) the feet of an animal that has four feet and claws

23

Index

Read more

Crossingham, John, and Bobbie Kalman. *The Life Cycle of a Raccoon.* New York: Crabtree (2003).

Nelson, Kristin L. *Clever Raccoons.* Minneapolis, MN: Lerner (2001).

Read, Tracy C. *Exploring the World of Raccoons.* Buffalo, NY: Firefly (2010).

Ripple, William John. *Raccoons.* Mankato, MN: Capstone (2006).

Learn more online

To learn more about raccoons, visit **www.bearportpublishing.com/WildBabyAnimals**

About the author

Ruth Owen has been writing children's books for more than ten years. She lives in Cornwall, England, just minutes from the ocean. Ruth loves gardening and caring for her family of llamas.